SOUND LEARNING

AND

RELIGIOUS EDUCATION

LECTURE DELIVERED AT THE KING'S COLLEGE
WOMEN'S DEPARTMENT, OCTOBER 5TH, 1904,

INTRODUCTORY TO THE
COURSES OF BIBLICAL STUDY

BY

ALICE GARDNER,

Lecturer and Associate of Newnham College, Cambridge.

T0382412

LONDON
C. J. CLAY AND SONS
CAMBRIDGE UNIVERSITY PRESS WAREHOUSE
AVE MARIA LANE
Glasgow: 50, WELLINGTON STREET
1904

CAMBRIDGE UNIVERSITY PRESS
Cambridge, New York, Melbourne, Madrid, Cape Town,
Singapore, São Paulo, Delhi, Mexico City

Cambridge University Press
The Edinburgh Building, Cambridge CB2 8RU, UK

Published in the United States of America by Cambridge University Press, New York

www.cambridge.org
Information on this title: www.cambridge.org/9781107677920

© Cambridge University Press 1904

First published 1904
Re-issued 2013

A catalogue record for this publication is available from the British Library

ISBN 978-1-107-67792-0 Paperback

SOUND LEARNING AND RELIGIOUS EDUCATION.

In choosing this venerable phrase for our starting-point to-day, I may possibly seem to be guilty of great presumption. For I have small enough personal claim myself to represent either of the great causes denoted in these words, nor should I venture, for the modest scheme we are about to launch, to demand the shelter of so notable an aegis. It is not as champions—rather as humble followers—that we would identify our ideal with that of the pioneers and promoters of learning and religion in all times. And there is no presumption in setting before us a lofty purpose, if we remember that it has belonged and still belongs to thousands of others who, in their pursuit of it, have attained very varying measures of success.

The juxtaposition of the two terms seemed to me suggestive of much that might lead to profitable reflections. Those of us who, in University churches or at certain cathedral services, have become familiar with this clause of the "bidding-prayer," may have sometimes felt it to arouse a melancholy feeling touched with a certain irony—or at least, incongruity. It is "in order that there may never be wanting a supply of men duly qualified to serve God both in Church and State" that we are bidden to "pray for a blessing on all seminaries of sound learning and religious education, particularly the Universities of this land." Without stopping to enquire whether the idea of capacity for service is in fact with us the main object of higher education, we cannot help believing that the clause which especially concerns us here represented in the minds of those who drew up the formula an intimate relation between learning—including what we should call science—and religion, considerably remote from present actuality. It is a relation which assumes that advance in what is called secular and in what is called religious knowledge should always be concomitant,—that every step made in intellectual progress should deepen and widen our ideas of religion ; and that all new light attained by the religious consciousness, every fresh stirring of religious zeal, should guide and stimulate the mind to the attainment of a higher plane of knowledge. Any rivalry or discord between the two great forces which raise men to the higher life does not appear as even conceivable. This is unfortunately *not* the modern view of the subject.

The historical reason of the change is not far to seek. Though the phrase may be of post-Reformation times, the idea is that of the Mediaeval Church. For that Church, not by reason of her innate character, nor of her original mission, but because of the political and social condition of things during the earlier centuries of her dominance, had become at one and the same time champion of learning against ignorance, of political order against brute force, and of morality against licence. If the literature and the cultured habits of the ancient world had survived, if there had been no barbarian invasions and no Mahometan propaganda, the Christian Church would still have had much to do, but in all probability neither the organizing of governments, nor the planting of agricultural institutions, nor yet the establishment of schools and libraries, the building up of the old materials and the new into an intellectual fabric unique in character—would ever have become her tasks. These suppositions, however, are beyond the reach of the most vigorous imagination. We must renounce the attempt at such flights, and contemplate the spectacle of primitive Christianity, struggling to vindicate itself as a " philosophy " in a cultured Pagan world, and in the Western Christianity of the Early Middle Ages, giving forth to barbarous peoples what it had assimilated—or sometimes perhaps clung to without assimilation — of ancient learning, generally in the forms which had been impressed upon it by the master-minds of the period of transition. With the Renaissance, if not earlier, a change was bound to come. The Church did not become less learned, but learning became strong enough to stand alone.

There is something very attractive and imposing in the unity of culture in Mediaeval Christendom, at least in Western Europe. But the Golden Age—whether or no we are to anticipate it in the future—is certainly nowhere to be found in the past. Learning was not necessarily pious because it dealt much with sacred things, any more than art is pious if fashion confines it to the depicting of Madonnas and Saints. Identity of dogmatic belief and even of religious observance was found to be compatible with the extreme types of moral excellence and depravity. Indeed I think we may say that neither then nor at any time has it been expedient for one of the two forces—learning or religion—to dominate the other. At that time, religion was all-powerful. And in the interests of religion itself, as well as in those of learning, the result was not altogether good. One hesitates to say anything in disparagement of periods which produced such lofty types of Christian character as Louis IX of France, Francis of Assisi, or the author of the *Imitatio*. Nor would we underrate the prodigious intellectual industry of those who raised the fabric of scholastic learning. "There were giants in the earth in those days." But those characters would have been still greater, because more natural, those labours would have been more fruitful, because more rational, if they had been more inspired by the breath of healthy human life, less over-shadowed by the terrors of the world to come. It may be objected that it is the tyranny of a one-sided type of religion rather than the all-pervading influence of religion itself of which I am complaining. But in reply I would suggest that any religion tends to become one-sided unless it is allowed to live and grow in the midst of ideas and interests of the kind we generally call secular. And many great minds have ever found an exclusively religious atmosphere uncongenial. We know how ecclesiastical authority has dealt with spirits whom reason had made recalcitrant. The examples of Abelard and Arnold of Brescia, of the Mediaeval Platonists, of many other obstinate questioners will occur to the mind. When Theology was Queen of the Sciences she had but a meagre realm, and many fertile fields were left uncultivated.

But we are quite secular enough nowadays, as few here are likely to dispute. Learning and religion go their several ways. Not only that learning is nowadays not very much regarded in Church appointments, except in rare cases. The halo which seemed to surround the seeker after truth has melted away, or lost any supramundane light. We hear a great deal about religious education, especially in the way of protest against religious education of some particular kind. But the most ardent champion in either educational camp would not as a rule venture to represent his cause as also that of good learning, any more than the foremost teachers of the sciences—human or natural—would assume the robes of a priest or the mantle of a prophet. There is not, perhaps, much of actual antagonism between religion and science— as generally understood—at the present day. Science has become wonderfully modest of late, in acknowledging its limitations and the vastness of the realms which lie beyond its boundaries, and it is more ready than ever before to treat as *fact* the experiences of the spiritual life. But we are far from having arrived at a clear mutual understanding between science and literary culture (which may for our present purposes be taken together) on the one hand, and religion on the other. This is bad for our religion, in keeping it narrow and unenlightened. It is also bad—if not for learning, yet for learned people—in excluding them from participating in some of the strongest helps to duty and perennial sources of happiness. Of course it does not shut them off from religious life in the highest sense. But it does deprive them in many cases of full religious communion with their fellows.

I should think it far worse than superfluous to enter here into a discussion of the conflict between the religious and the learned influences in our modern life. But as we need to see the origin of the dissension before we can take even the humblest means towards removing it, I may just point out what seems to be, historically, the cause of the difficulty. Religion must always "speak as one having authority." Mediaeval learning was based on authority also, on tradition accumulated and interpreted according to traditional canons. Modern learning is critical, and its methods are the scientific ones of observation and inductive reasoning. In early times—in all times—there is bound to be a conflict between rival authorities, but, generally speaking, the authorities formerly recognized were more or less of one kind. The authority to which mediaeval learning bowed was that which spoke also in the Church. But modern learning knows no authority save the consensus of experts. There have, of course, been visionary schemes of a really effective religious authority established on a scientific basis. But any such scheme is, to say the least, remote, and in the interests of liberty and progress we can hardly wish to see it among us set on a firm footing.

The separation thus marked out may appear beyond hope of reunion. Our religious faith must be something well beyond reach of intellectual controversies, disputed texts, or metaphysical fogs. "Religion," says Matthew Arnold, "must be something about which there is no puzzle." (He would not, of course, have said "no mystery.") And knowledge could not flourish—nay, she would not continue to live—if she had to submit to any laws but those which she had herself sanctioned. What is the plain man to do who feels the need of religion and is yet, in common honesty, bound to recognize the claims of knowledge?

Whatever he does, if he is a plain, honest man he is bound to make no compromise, but to acknowledge to the full the claims of both. I do not say that the plain man will always see exactly where he is to bow to the authority of religion and where to follow the conclusions of his reason or of reasonable investigation. But he may at least be taught not to go a little way in one direction and then, if the path becomes encumbered and stiff, leap over the wall into another road. If he has decided that the validity, for him, of certain religious doctrines and observances rests on a higher than human authority, he has no right to cease to meditate on the doctrine or to practise the observances in consequence of any changes that increased knowledge may have brought about in his theories as to their origin. Or if he submits certain questions of fact or of argument about which he has strong religious feelings to be decided by the ordinary methods of historical or critical science, he is not at liberty, if he finds the case going as he would wish it not to go, to fall back on authority and declare that the point at issue is a matter of faith. It was in his power to say this at the first. Like Ananias, he is keeping back part of the price. If he is only a plain man, we should be too harsh if we went on to say to him—as we may fairly say to thinking people who do this advisedly—that they have lied, not unto men, but unto God.

But I fear that I am becoming at once too abstract and too censorious. I would acknowledge that in these regions we all of us, however honestly minded, trip occasionally. And if I seem merely to have stated an insoluble problem, I would answer cheerfully, *solvitur ambulando*. We may never reach a conclusion quite satisfactory in itself. But in our efforts towards a practical line of conduct we may hope for the light which comes soon or late to all honest seekers.

For after all, human life is not divided into so many quite distinct compartments, with no communication between them. The divisions which might seem impenetrable, are but the cell-walls of a living organism. Our thoughts and our beliefs about religion and about other matters are determined by the same deep, underlying causes. And even where we must draw the line, it is found to be elastic. To put this matter more literally: although it is desirable to make the distinction in our minds between spiritual and intellectual authority, yet we practically find that the kind of subjects which we refer to one or the other depends very much on our mind and character, and especially that the extent of the sphere allowed to intellectual authority increases immensely with the development of intellectual culture and scientific habits of mind, whereas that of the purely spiritual judgment grows in strength but not necessarily in compass with the growth in religious depth and sincerity.

Thus I think we now find the principle generally accepted by all educated and thoughtful people who have to discuss questions of evidence and proof, that no divine voice has ever authoritatively assured man of any things as to which his ordinary faculties were competent to decide. This principle was not grasped in the ages during which man had not learned how far his faculties availed him and where they broke down. And it is just in those particular regions where any one student has attained fixed principles and well tested results that he is most unwilling to accept, on spiritual authority, any statement that is evidently at variance with his special conclusions or general theory. In departments of knowledge with which he is unfamiliar, he is probably indifferent as to whether such higher authority is to be accepted or not. For us whose knowledge of most things is generally not first-hand, it has become habitual to look for information to those who are best informed, and not to expect a divine revelation coming along the lines by which human knowledge is visibly progressing. At the same time it is possible while questioning or denying the obligation to accept any statements on matters of science or history on purely religious grounds, to acknowledge most fully the significance which a religious interpretation may give to any kind of truth, however obtained.

These principles will, I hope, become clearer after we have considered a little the subject in which they chiefly need to be applied: that of the study of the Bible.

The study of the Bible provides a large meeting-ground— I fear I must add a battle-field,—for all motive and principles that may ever have impelled and regulated the pursuit of sound learning and of religious education. The Bible is accepted among us as the handbook—in all Christian countries as the main source—of religious instruction. At the same time, since it is a book of composite structure, of various and remote dates, both in language and thought containing very much that is almost unintelligible to modern minds, describing and indicating conditions of society veiled in obscurity but of great historical interest—it has, quite apart from the sanction of religious authority, a unique importance for the student of mankind. And all except a few uncultivated fanatics allow the necessity of at least some serious intellectual effort and the application of knowledge derived from various regions for an appreciation—except of the rudest kind—of even the spiritual teaching of Biblical writers. Nevertheless there seems to be a general consensus among educated people that the Bible does not hold so prominent a place as it ought to do, in our education and our reading. I speak of a general consensus—but this is true only as to the negative side of the complaint, since there is by no means a consensus as to the place which the Bible *ought* to hold among us. But even this narrow ground of unanimity gives us, at least, a starting-point of enquiry: why is not the Bible taught more thoroughly in schools, and read more intelligently at home?

Chiefly, I would answer, because of the great confusion in the public mind as to what Bible study is, how it should be carried on, and what may be expected from it. This confusion is, of course, in itself a proof of the deficiency complained of and a full justification of the complaint. The fact briefly and baldly stated is that a large section of the British public is nervous of Biblical study except on such conditions as would strangle the growth of any study worth the name. It does not always know exactly *why* it is nervous, but I think we may resolve the cause of dread into two elements: people are afraid that Bible teaching will be mixed up with "views," and in different sections of the public there are different sets of views regarded as spiritually dangerous; and in the second place they have some dread lest the habit of taking up the Bible according to modern methods of free enquiry might lead to the loss of its unique position in our estimation,—lest the spirit of "sound learning" should entirely crush, or at least inflict serious damage on, the cause of religious education.

Now I believe that there is, if not a sound justification, a very plausible pretext for both these fears. They imply considerable haziness of thought; they suppose the necessary persistence of influences which some of us are trying to reduce considerably, if not to eliminate, and if either of them were to be allowed full scope, such an enterprise as that we are beginning to-day would be doomed from the outset. But they are so widespread, even among cultivated and intellectual people, that we must give them a little consideration.

Now as to the connection of Biblical Teaching with particular religious views, it would be absurd to deny its existence. Yet all who have followed with interest and attention for twenty or thirty years the progress of educated opinion on the subject must allow that, as was said just now, the sphere allowed, within the range of Biblical studies, to the ordinary methods of explanation and criticism, has been of late immensely increased. Educated people have long become accustomed to a far freer use than our fathers would have sanctioned as to Old Testament narratives and even Old Testament standards of common morals. We are inclined to smile at the attitude of a man like Professor Freeman, who, as late as his undergraduate days, denied, on the authority of Scripture, the rotundity of the earth. No philologist is accused of heresy for looking elsewhere than to the Tower of Babel for the origin of languages and dialects. The standing-still of the sun at the desire of Joshua does not worry us; even the sneer of Gibbon as to the silence of the ancient world on the darkness of the Passion seems to us beneath the notice of a Christian apologist. Where physical science and statements of Holy Writ have come into close conflict, science has been victorious all along the line,—one need hardly say without any loss to the prestige of the Bible. It seems to me that we owe more than we always acknowledge to the reputation of those earnest scholars who by their efforts, at the cost of much disapproval and resistance, even from those who ought to have trusted and supported them, have earned for us the promised land of freedom into which they entered not in themselves. We do not accept all their conclusions nor follow out all their principles. Some of those principles appear to us entirely unsound—such as the cumbersome and unactual process of allegorizing, by which very often the plain sense of plain narratives was skilfully explained away. Some of their generalizations were crude, just because it was impossible to bring them into connection with hosts of facts that have since been discovered. But if the allegorizers seem timid and shifty, if the destructive critics were too hasty, is there no timidity, nor shiftiness, nor haste among our scholars of to-day? Let us pay due honour to the pioneers whose faces were turned towards the light, yet consider that if we go no further than they went we are guilty of the reproach made against those who built the sepulchres of the prophets but followed not their teaching.

After all, however, it may be said that those questions as to which free enquiry is allowed by all except a few extremists are far less important than those as to which there are deeply-lying differences. And it has become, in education, a recognized principle that no teacher ought to give instruction that conflicts with religious doctrine in which his pupils are being brought up, while in the case of adults, conflicts of the kind are commonly—and often rightly—regarded as undesirable. To take first the case of children—of course the matter would be simple if the line, which we have already called an elastic one—between matters of faith and of knowledge were more clearly drawn, though for the good of all in the present state of culture I cannot say that I desire to see it made altogether definite. With respect to the regions of which I have already spoken, those which have been frankly given over to historical and critical determination, there are, of course, some parents who have not grasped the situation. Suppose the child of such parents came home saying, "Miss Dash told us that the Jews didn't have the laws to keep till ever so long after Moses," or, "Mr Blank says that he doesn't think St John wrote all his Gospel himself," and if the parents take alarm and complain, what is to be done? It may be said that careful teachers will know how to avoid such situations, but certainly they can only do so by discouraging children from freely asking questions—a procedure not only at variance with our present educational notions, but additionally pernicious here as tending to provoke suspicion in the enquiring mind of a clever child. If the teacher gives way, it will be a case—the only one possible, perhaps, in our educational system—of ignorance dictating to knowledge. If he stands out, he will contradict the principle of parental rights over religious instruction. The only course open will be, first to try to convince the parent that he is not teaching anything dangerous, or opposed to such authorities in the Church or in literature as the parent would approve, and if the attempt fails, to let the child be withdrawn from religious instruction altogether. This very undesirable extreme can, I believe, be in most cases avoided, since even uncultured and narrow-minded parents are susceptible of the impression made by an earnest and high-minded teacher. And the teacher may console himself with the thought that if a few pupils are withdrawn and a certain unpopularity incurred by his honesty and thoroughness, yet a far more important set of young minds is likely to obtain from him a living interest in the Bible, which the others may, after all, derive from their Church or Sunday-school.

For a greater danger seems to me to lie in the loss of familiarity with the Bible on the part of children of a different type of parents,—those who would allow the maximum, rather than the minimum of extent to rational and natural investigation and interpretation of Scripture. We probably know many parents such as these. There are some who, with a love and reverence for the Bible, have broken finally with the current popular theology, and who regretfully let their children grow up without knowledge of the Scriptures rather than let them acquire such knowledge as part and parcel of a body of thought which they have themselves rejected. Such parents may or may not take their children to church, or read the Bible with them at home, but even if they do both, listening to reading without instruction and explanation does not generally make very much impression on the average child, and in most cases the parents feel that they have not sufficient knowledge to teach the children adequately, so that, unless good school teaching is to be had, the result is ignorance. There are other parents equally free in thought whose pursuits have lain in other fields and who have but a slight and vague appreciation of the Bible, yet who would not object to letting their children learn it, if they could be sure that there was not on the part of the teacher even an unconscious inclination to make the teaching dogmatic. Such children would, I believe, even more than the others, profit by Biblical teaching with the minimum of doctrinal instruction.

Now the practical question is : can the Bible be profitably and reverently taught to the children of free-thinkers (I use the word in no invidious sense) and to the children of ordinary Christians by the same teachers and in the same classes? I know that there are great differences of opinion on this point, but quite believe that it is possible, though I should say that it required, on the part of the teacher, great tact and discernment, with a large measure of faith (though to some the word may sound strange in this connection), and certainly with a far sounder and wider knowledge of the subject than most of our women-teachers have, as yet, had opportunity of acquiring. A teacher in such a position would have to be careful to make his class know, as far as possible, what the Biblical writers said and what was their meaning at the time ; not what their words have, by the interpretations of various Churches and schools, been taken to mean, even if lawfully and profitably, for later generations; he would relate as events, what seemed, according to the most reasonable interpretation of data, to have happened, with care to recognize our great uncertainty as to a great many events that we would willingly give our little fingers to know about, and the possibility of more than one historical hypothesis being accepted on good grounds by different people. He would not hesitate to speak of progress and of occasional decline in morals and religion. Scriptural characters he would try to treat in such a way as to make them seem living persons and to call forth admiration for great achievements, sympathy with noble efforts, regret for the failings of even good men. Of the Central Character of all he would speak as becomes one who feels that the study of it would well fill many life-times, and he would do all he could to make the social and physical environment of that figure form for it a clear background; he would allow the imagination of his pupils to play around the Gospel narrative, as the imagination of Christendom has done through all the ages. And if he succeeded in making the human character appeal in its human dignity and beauty, he need run no risk of in any way distressing or confusing those pupils who are at the same time being taught to regard it as divine.

It will be objected that the liberal human view of the Bible cannot be given to young children, that they must have something definite and plain or nothing at all. But I appeal to all who have ever tried to teach historical or literary subjects to intelligent children, whether they have not found it quite possible and most interesting to instil into them some notions of the care we have to take to avoid thinking that we know all the truth about anything, and of the great differences —yet differences that by no means shut out from human fellowship—between the men of old time and the men of to-day. And I would appeal to all who have given religious instruction to children, or who have themselves first been taught the Bible from the point of view of popular and conventional theology, whether a new breath of life is not wanted to give actuality to the whole story in children's minds—a breath that can only come from the spirit of the historically-guided, truth-loving, sympathetic imagination. I know not whether the experience of others is like my own. But I believe that thousands of children cannot possibly love or even actualize the historical Christ, because He has never been presented to them in a natural and simple way.

In the case of adults, who have taken the responsibility of their intellectual and religious culture into their own hands, these remarks only apply to a limited extent. The adult, in setting about Biblical study, has not to think of the scruples of any third party (like the parents whom we have imagined as standing between teacher and pupils). At the same time the adult has probably views of his own, and he may often think that his regard for those views ought to confine his reading to works written by people who share his persuasions. Now it might at first seem as if such hesitation were to be condemned as cowardly, since every person of robust mind ought to be eager to let in light and air from all quarters. Yet unfortunately we have not all of us very robust minds, and the number of books we can read is necessarily limited, so that it is often advisable for us to select our books, and yet more the order in which we should read them, with a view primarily to our powers of assimilating the good and rejecting the useless. These powers depend a good deal on our sympathy with the writers, a sympathy which sometimes, though not always, involves identity of religious opinions. Thus some people may feel that they can learn very little from those who belong to other schools and Churches than their own. Such people are, of course, less happy and less likely to obtain great acquisition of knowledge than are those whose net is more widely spread. But till they have obtained a greater receptivity of mind and power of discrimination between the essential and the accidental elements in their own religious life and thought, no one would advise them to give themselves useless labour in grappling with what they are not able to conquer. We must all of us progress gradually, and in our progress we must avail ourselves of the help of those whom we find best able to help us. Even if our favourite teachers are not the men of the very soundest learning, their teaching may be the best for us at any particular time, provided of course that their learning is really sound and progressive, and their minds set on the attainment of truth and not on any inferior aim.

These considerations bring us to our second hindrance in the way of thorough Biblical study—the suspicion lest such study should arrogate to itself too large a sphere ; lest sound learning should usurp all the claims and all the functions of religious education.

Now in order that we may do what we want to do we are bound not to promise or to attempt too much. It may be necessary, though it should be quite superfluous, to insist that

the most enlightened, conscientious, and appreciative study of
the Bible or of any other books can never stand in lieu of
direct religious and moral training of children, nor of spiritual
discipline for the adult. Such a conception seems to show
the old confusion between instruction and education. Education includes instruction, but it takes in a good deal more,
since it comprises, besides the imparting of knowledge and
the development of the intellectual powers, the yet greater
task of building up character. Of course, since man is a
rational being, there must be a strong intellectual element in
this work of construction. No character, however refined and
lofty, is stable without settled principles, which the mind has
recognized though it may not have discovered them. But
beyond the inculcation of principle there is a wide non-
rational—I do not say irrational—field in the formation of
habits and the cultivation of the conscience. And, partly
through constant appeal to principle, partly through training
in regular habits, still more by the setting forth of ideals and
the culture of the higher moral feelings—of admiration and
love for the excellent, of scorn for all that is mean and low—
a real educator may accomplish much that would be impossible to him if he confined himself to the work of a teacher.
For he creates about him what Mr Balfour calls a "psycho-
logical atmosphere" favourable to his main object.

From what I have already said it will be seen that I do
not consider the teacher adequate to his task unless he is
capable of doing more than directly imparting knowledge,
though that in itself is no trivial and easy task. But what I
wanted to insist upon was that though the Bible, or parts of
it, may and should be used as the manual of religious instruction, yet religious education involves, besides knowledge of
the book, a training in religious habits, a reverence for
religious ideals, and, generally speaking, life in an atmosphere
in which all that belongs to the higher life of man can live
and grow, all that is mean and sordid must vanish away. The
inadequacy of Scripture teaching alone to achieve this desider-
atum has been set forth in racy if somewhat extravagant style
by Mr Charles Marson, a Somersetshire clergyman, in a little

paper called "Huppim and Muppim, a few words on the sore need of religious education," to which I would refer you for a somewhat extreme view of the case.

His contention is that nowadays everybody is anxious to have children taught the whole Bible story, from "the earth without form and void" to the "second missionary journey of St Paul," including especially the interesting fact that "the sons of Benjamin were Huppim and Muppim and Ard," while very few people care at all that children should be taught to follow the most important services of the Church to which they are supposed to belong. With the negative side of this brochure I have a good deal of sympathy. There is certainly nothing more of the nature of religious education about the sons of Benjamin than about those of Edward III or King Priam. Personally, however, I think that our elementary teachers, with all their shortcomings, are not so absolutely without sense of proportion as to lay stress on points of this kind. But the tract is good as a *reductio ad absurdum* of notions the absurdity of which is not generally recognized. If we try to get all our moral and religious teaching from the Bible, even if we avoid the worst extravagances, we are likely to lay too heavy a meaning on some words of Scripture and to give the whole a non-natural aspect, since, in reading it with children, we feel bound to draw some moral or religious lesson from every story. I do not share the opinion of some that the modern child objects to morals at the end of stories. I believe that he looks for them in some places, as in Aesop's fables, and is disappointed if they are not there. But to see a moral meaning in a story and to put a moral in for the purpose of drawing it out are two very different processes. The moral and religious education of children should, in so far as it is connected with their Bible lessons, be bound up with the study of chosen passages, and it should not be derived from the Bible only.

I would here mention one point the following up of which would lead us somewhat afield : the great want at the present day, of rational instruction in the elementary principles of right and wrong. Moral, or rather ethical, teaching has suffered from our general dread of the critical attitude as to matters in which humility and obedience to authority are all-important. And the result is a general haze in most people's minds as to the most essential principles of morals. For example, in teaching young people and in ordinary conversation, I am often struck with the incapacity of most persons to give the reason why; *e.g.* they condemn gambling or insist on certain minor duties; and there comes from this theoretical haziness a great want of practical security in determining the line between the permitted and the prohibited. Of course in many cases, moral instincts, strengthened by good habits, lead aright. But the categorical imperative has often a conditional clause, and want of reasonable and habitual reflection on conduct makes a harmonious and well-directed life a rare phenomenon among us. Now I do not feel inclined to draw any strong line between morals and religion, and to insist that children should be taught on a purely secular system of ethics. Religious ideals and standards, and religious helps to duty cannot be omitted unless the whole subject is to be treated on a narrower scale and a lower plane. But to allow an appeal to such ideals and helps in the discussion of morals, and to base *all* morals on the texts and documents of canonical books are two very different things. The Bible is able to furnish illustrations in abundance of the chief moral principles that any good ethical teacher would lay down, and it is superfluous to say that one would always naturally have recourse to it from the expression of the highest moral teaching. But on the one hand, certain portions of the Bible cannot be adequately studied simply as media of moral teaching, and on the other hand, much instruction that is sorely needed on the practical duties of modern life is not explicitly—though it may be implicitly—taught in the Scriptures. I leave the question whether distinct moral lessons ought or ought not to be given in schools. But I feel very strongly that whether as a separate lesson or not, children should be taught to think seriously about moral distinctions, and that their moral judgment should be trained to work more independently than it can possibly do if confined to the definite application of precepts from Holy Scripture.

As to religious education pure and simple, the clergyman
I have quoted would apparently base much of it on the
practice and explanation of Christian ritual. This is like the
old Jewish way: "When thy son asketh thee...what meaneth
this? then thou shalt say" and so forth. At the same time,
as was remarked to me by an anthropologist, this is just the
way in which the old mythologies were built up,—from the
explanation—adequate or not—of ritual. I do not think that
Christian ritual—except where it is far more complex than it
is in most churches—would be much better able to bear the
strain than the Bible narrative taken as it stands. But I do
not wish to say how it should be done. The great thing is
for the teacher to set an ideal before him, and to have as
much scope as possible in choosing his own ways of pursuing
it. Any of us who in childhood or youth have had lessons
in religion from religious people know how in these matters
"the wind bloweth as it listeth," and we must allow scope for
diversity of character, powers, and circumstances, and trust to
what we must generally come to rely on ultimately, the individual impress of a devout spirit. In this sense it is perhaps
true that religious education should be left to the home and
the Church, and only to teachers in so far as they stand to
the children in *loco parentis* or in the position of spiritual
guardians. But, after all, teachers very often are in such a position. This is, however, a question beyond our present inquiry.

With regard to adults, the confusion is slightly different,
but fundamentally not unlike. As some teachers would—
according to Mr Marson—find religious education for children
in statements concerning the sons of Benjamin, so many people
who have taken their education—or discipline—into their own
hands, have sometimes thought that they might seek the good
of their souls by studies no more spiritually inspiring than
that of Huppim, Muppim, and Ard. But the fault was not in
the studies, only in what was expected from them. We all
need, occasionally, some word of power to shame us out of
our lassitude and strengthen us to walk on in confidence and
hope. Many of us, too, may have dark times when the world
seems an empty show and our lives but bubbles on a fleeting
torrent, rushing we know not whither. And at all times of

our lives we—or almost all of us—need some seasons of with-
drawal from the seen and temporal to contemplate the unseen
and eternal. Now any worthy and ennobling study is able to
act as a counteractive to languor, to depression, to frivolity.
But Biblical investigation cannot directly and immediately
afford the relief and stimulus we require. Not to learn new
things, but thoroughly to realize what we know already;—
not the study of ancient records, but the application of eternal
truth to present individual needs; not the training in habits
of methodical reasoning, but the power,—also acquired through
habit—to throw away distractions and to lay hold of the
spiritual helps that are always at hand: these are the objects
of religious discipline to those who believe in it and according
to their power seek to practise it.

Some may think that I am giving our case away:—for to
most people the personal and devotional use of the Bible is
the only use that they care to have, and to use it in any other
way is to divert it from its proper purpose. But I am ready
to maintain that the practical and spiritual influence of the
Bible is likely not only to remain unimpaired but to be greatly
enhanced by the theoretical and intellectual appreciation of
its contents. And I would go on to say that even this intellectual appreciation is of very high spiritual value.

Of course it is true that critical study often gives such a
different significance to passages or books of the Bible from
those formerly held as to dissever them from many beautiful
and helpful ideas formerly associated with them. I suppose
that a good deal of very exalted feeling has in some mystic
readers been stimulated by meditations on the Song of
Solomon, such as we cannot enter into nowadays. That
book is read by few and enjoyed by still fewer. It is a
difficult work for us, not because we have to discover hidden
meanings in every verse, but because we find it hard to discover the several parts of the various dramatis personae, and
harder still to distinguish, in its imagery, the elements of
Oriental sensuousness and of pure and passionate love. Few
of us would either seek or find spiritual help in it. But if a
critical tone and a historical judgment cause us to lose in

some quarters, how much do they make us gainers in others! How full of meaning do many chapters in St Paul's Epistles become to us when we study the Apostle as a real historical character, in relation to the circumstances and also the thought of his time! I would go further and say that many of the words of his Master come home with fresh force to the minds of those who have tried to follow His footsteps, as humble disciples it may well be, but also as students.

The very notion that the Bible should lose influence through critical examination seems to show not only a distrust of the Bible itself, but a poor opinion of the whole character of modern scholarship. If we look at the nearest analogies we can find (of course no book is in a position closely analogous to that of the Bible) we do not find that critical study of the greatest books has lowered their estimate. How much change has come over our notions of the Homeric poems! Here we have discoveries of composite authorship, disbelief in historicity of narrative, numberless questions raised as to points of language, customs, ideas of gods and men. Yet never before to-day has Homer been realized as so rich a storehouse of multifarious knowledge, and no less now than ages ago is he powerful to stir the feelings and to kindle the imagination. Are Plato, Dante, Shakespeare less admired and loved because they are read more critically than of yore? But probably an objector would say that he has no fear lest the Bible should not stand criticism, but considerable misgivings as to the effect on the mind of the reader of assuming towards it a critical attitude. Such misgivings would naturally arise from the unhappy identification of criticism with carping and disparagement, a view only too well justified by much that passes for criticism at the present day. But if it is the business of the critic to "prove all things" and "hold fast that which is good," criticism is likely to make all that is good more evident and more potent than it could be in a dull atmosphere of unquestioning ignorance.

Again, reasonable criticism may remove many hindrances to the moral appreciation of the Bible. We frequently come across simple and uninstructed people who are puzzled or shocked in reading of the murders committed by Jael and by Jehu, the crude ideas of the Deity shown in some of the Psalms, the mistake of the Apostles in expecting the immediate return of their Lord. Biblical study does not meet all these difficulties face to face, but it generally leads the student to a position whence he can contemplate them from a higher standpoint. Under its guidance he finds it natural that religious growth, in nations as in individuals, should be gradual, and that spiritual rectitude should sometimes be accompanied by moral or intellectual limitations. The attempt to force the moral sense into acquiescence with the supposed teaching of Scripture has often led to strange aberrations which wider knowledge might have avoided.

But apart from the most directly practical considerations, sound learning in Biblical subjects has an invigorating and purifying power which we may surely regard as a spiritual gain. It shares that power with all good learning whatsoever, but possesses it in a specially full measure. The value of all learning is twofold, it trains our faculties and it puts us in possession of new realms of thought. Apply this test to the study of the Bible. Do we or do we not exercise and develope our faculties worthily when we are trying to understand the meaning of prophets and apostles? And are the worlds revealed to us by enlightened Biblical study worth possessing or are they not? It would be presumptuous to answer these questions at length, and happily it is quite superfluous.

I would add a word or two about the different kinds of students and different studies contemplated by those who are developing our still tentative scheme. We have had in view very prominently the requirements of women teachers. I need not repeat the arguments by which we have been urging the necessity of a higher standard of knowledge than has heretofore prevailed among those who have to teach Scripture as a class subject in schools. I would only make one more remark: that we hope in time to see such a recognition of the importance of thorough Biblical study as may encourage some future teachers to devote much more time and attention to it than is involved in following a few courses of lectures. Not that

I wish to see many women specializing in Divinity at our Universities, though I think it would be an excellent thing for students to take after finishing some other course, *e.g.* one part of the Cambridge Theological Tripos or the B.D. course at London University. Over-specializing is to be deprecated in most subjects, and in Divinity, which really requires a certain breadth of culture, it is more pernicious than anywhere else. The late Canon Ainger used to say to young students of theology : " If you are nothing but divines, you are very bad divines." But there is for us just now far less danger from the narrowness of the specialist than from the superficiality of the amateur. I do not think the standard of Scripture teaching in girls' schools will ever be satisfactory until some at least of the mistresses take it up for a time as their chief subject. In school teaching the New Testament should, of course, be a more prominent subject than the Old, and no teacher should be regarded as fit to undertake advanced classes unless she has made some study of it in Greek, and can at least find her way about in standard works of reference for linguistic and historical difficulties. A school in which Scripture is made a prominent subject and yet has no one mistress in it capable of reading the New Testament in the original, seems to me almost as great an anomaly as a school laying great stress upon modern literature, in which the teachers can only read Dante and Goethe in translations.

For women of leisure who are reading with no ulterior object beyond their own profit and enjoyment, the provision to be made will probably in general be the same as for teachers, since if subjects have to be taught, it is presumed that they are worth learning ;—else all our education would run in a vicious circle. Of course there would be the difference, that persons of leisure might take up by preference some attractive side-subjects for which the professional teacher had no time. But though the following up of by-ways is by no means to be discouraged, it is best undertaken by those who know the direction of the main roads. In plain language, I hope that when a definite and continuous course is made out, it will be taken up by many who are not bound to keep to the lines, but who feel that the work is likely to be more thorough and satisfactory if they do so.

We have also kept in view the needs of those who intend to become instructors in Christian knowledge of non-Christian or semi-Christian adults,—our own poor and the populations of heathen countries. For both kinds of mission work it is quite clear that a pretty high standard both of knowledge and of skill in dealing with difficult questions is needed at the present day ;—perhaps it was needed in former days, but was not to be had. Everyone who has glanced at the lower class of secularist newspapers, whence the British workman largely derives his opinions on religious and other subjects, must have noticed how the anti-religious point of view is taken up chiefly through such ignorance and prejudice as should be met by the presentation of truth in all " sweet reasonableness " and freshness of mind rather than by well-meant but hasty and perhaps illogical denunciation of error. This is a very large subject. The estrangement of what is called "the masses " from all the Churches presents a sad and humiliating spectacle to those who can take it to heart. I do not say that the utmost that any band of individuals can do in studying the principles of Christianity as set forth in the Bible or in the teachings of life and history can go very far. Still if it goes any way at all, it is on the path which seems marked out in clear Christian duty.

With regard also to foreign and colonial missions, it has become evident to almost all directors of missionary societies, that besides religious zeal, a very considerable amount of knowledge is required in those who endeavour either to meet the intellectual arguments and aspirations of educated heathens or to grasp the strangely rudimentary conceptions of the savage mind. Everybody knows that mistakes have often been made by devoted but insufficiently equipped missionaries. Rude barbarians must be approached carefully, not treated as if they had the minds of twentieth century Englishmen. As to civilized nations with ancient systems of thought and cult, one feels at times a strong desire that if they are to be led to adopt Christianity in some form suitable to their character and history, they might be spared some of the very undesirable phases through which European Christianity has had to pass. It is no easy task to distinguish in modern Christianity what is due to the original data, to lawful and healthy development, and to unhealty accretion. Very much that has been cumbersome to our fathers and to us may well be dispensed with for other nations, so as to bring gain rather than loss to what is living and essential. All the learning and culture we can obtain will fall short of solving the problem entirely—but anything that we can learn by devoted study will help us towards a practical line of thought and policy.

I am not without hopes that the knowledge acquired here may lead to the future existence of another class of students,—of women engaged not in the diffusion but in the advancement of Biblical learning. Very few women have as yet taken any part in Biblical research, either of a textual or critical kind, but there are some, and their example may encourage others.

As to the subjects to be here offered : it must be borne in mind that our general scheme is not as yet completed and our present effort is merely tentative. We are offering Courses of Lectures on various fields of Biblical study—and of some cognate subjects—without as yet laying down any order in which the Courses should be taken. There are two courses on Biblical Study pure and simple, such as I should hope would always form the backbone of the scheme, though I should also hope that more difficult and advanced book teaching will be required as time goes on. One of these is on the books of the Old Testament, the other on those of the New; and in connection there will be classes in New Testament Greek and in elementary Hebrew. I hope that those who feel drawn to Old Testament studies will try to acquire some knowledge of Hebrew. Speaking for myself, I feel that the want of such knowledge prevents me from obtaining a satisfactory grip on subjects that require acquaintance with the original text, and if I had the freedom, youth, and leisure, I should certainly take it up now. But of course knowledge of the Greek Testament stands in quite another category. It is within the reach of every young woman who has had a good school education; and for understanding the documents of the Christian religion, it is clearly a necessity, while Hebrew is but a very desirable luxury.

There is also to be a course on Church History. I have very long felt how a sound knowledge of this subject, and especially the power to look at Church questions from a historical point of view, might be of immense service to us in allaying the bitterness that often prevails among various religious bodies, and narrows our conceptions to those of a small set of people. At the same time I do not regard with all confidence a recent movement to secure the recognition of Church History as a school subject, because I feel that unless the teachers have real accuracy of knowledge and breadth of sympathy, and withal a thoroughly historical tone of mind, they are likely to achieve results exactly the opposite of what I should desire. Church History, it seems to me, should always be taught in close connection with other kinds of history. Mankind is organic, and you can no more separate his religious ideas, impulses, and actions from his general political and social life than, in studying physiology, you can take the skeleton quite apart from the muscular system, or *vice versâ*. Though of course we need to have experts both in bones and muscles; and all students of the subject have to give special attention to one or other department in turn, Ecclesiastical History is a subject well worth special study, though it is not the best kind of history for a beginner.

Besides these subjects, two courses are to be given of a more abstract or philosophical kind, one kindly offered by the Principal of King's College, which deals with Christian Doctrine, and another of a more general nature. Persons beginning these subjects are often attracted to the abstract rather than the concrete from the very natural desire to arrive at broad generalizations, and to go down to the fundamental principles of human knowledge. It seems to me that for most of us a combination of abstract and concrete is desirable in order to keep the mental balance true. Those who have only to do with facts are apt to view them in isolation and so never attain to a rational comprehension of them. Those too eager to generalize are only too likely to form hasty generalizations on insufficient data, and, for want of a firm footing of experimental knowledge, to depart from the realms of actuality altogether. But without forcing any minds to a prolonged sojourn in uncongenial climates, we would try to avoid that anybody's learning should become one-sided. In neither sphere is there a short-cut to the truth. Patience and independence of mind are needed in all work, but most conspicuously in work of an abstract kind.

A word in conclusion to the kind friends who have shown sympathy with us in our plans and projects. We rely very much on the cooperation of all those whose objects even in part are coincident with ours, and such cooperation will, we hope, take the form of free suggestions and criticisms, so that we may never feel ignorant as to how our designs are practically working out. It must necessarily happen that there is a great diversity of views and aims among those to whom the promotion of Biblical Study among women seems a cause worthy of much earnest thought and concentrated effort. If—as must sometimes be the case—we differ in details, let us realize that we all have common enemies to strive against : —ignorance and indifference, and that genuine zeal for knowledge should outweigh many defects, intellectual or spiritual, among those whom it unites in cordial goodwill.

And so we launch our little bark in hope, not anticipating that she will speedily bring us in treasure from many climes, but trusting that she will enable many to visit fair fields and noble cities, and to gain health and vigour in pure and high atmospheres. Even if she should not long prove sea-worthy our travellers would at least have profited by her while she lasted. But some of us may be allowed to indulge the hope that the movement, of which our present effort is a humble part, may lead to great results. For it may help to bring on the day when "sound learning and religious education" will once more appear as naturally and inseparably associated together, not by means of compromise and reservations, but by a worthier conception of human life, and a surer light on the path which leads to the full satisfaction of both the intellectual and the spiritual needs of man.

For EU product safety concerns, contact us at Calle de José Abascal, 56–1°,
28003 Madrid, Spain or eugpsr@cambridge.org.